MW01232713

THE

CONFIDENCE

TO SPEAK

Kirk House Publishers

THE CONFIDENCE TO SPEAK

Master the Many Fears of Speaking

Sara Krisher

The Confidence to Speak Copyright © 2020 Sara Krisher

All rights reserved. This book or any portion thereof may not be reproduced or used in any manner whatsoever without the express written permission of the publisher except for the use of brief quotations in a book review.

Printed by Kirk House Publishers, in the United States of America.

First printing, November 2020

ISBN: 978-1-952976-06-3
LOC: 2020919898

Kirk House Publishers
1250 East 115th Street
Burnsville, MN 55337
Kirkhousepublishers.com

For Neal and Danika, the loves of my life:
Thank you for believing in me even when
I didn't believe in myself.

Table of Contents

Foreword

Not long ago, I was told I would be honored with an award at an upcoming event. Along with receiving the award, I was asked to deliver a speech—to share insights about my company's growth and my leadership journey. In my role as president, I often speak to groups, teams, and audiences, but somehow this was different. I was being recognized before an audience of incredibly talented business leaders and felt pressure to not only be an exemplary communicator on stage, but to be bold in my presence. I knew I needed help.

Sara was referred to me by my productivity coach, Jan Lehman, who I deeply respect. I wasn't sure what to expect but feared the typical lesson on how to make better eye contact and stop saying "um," all while being recorded. After meeting Sara, with her larger-than-life smile, I knew her training was something special. I was in good hands.

Running a multimillion-dollar company has taught me many valuable lessons. I've learned the answers don't always come easy, the writing is rarely ever on the wall, and that if you pay close attention, you will recognize opportunities that present themselves. Of course, we still do our due diligence, we project what the future holds, and we work the plan, but the magic is not in the spreadsheets and business plans. The magic required to innovate and maintain a growth mindset and positive culture consistently presents itself in the form of opportunity, which can come at any time. Our job as leaders is to recognize the opportunity. When it taps you on the shoulder, you look toward it.

The same can be said for speaking. Sara made it possible for me to create a plan for what to say. I learned how to deliver the message and about the importance of practice, but more importantly, she emphasized the need to always leave room for opportunity. The magic of a presentation is not in the perfectly prepared slide deck, the carefully chosen words, or the alluring finesse one has on stage. She taught me how to be authentic and in the moment so I could connect with my audience. She challenged me to take the stage without notes or a slide deck and just tell my story, in my own words. The magic in speaking is in the connected experience. Everything else is a bonus.

When the day came to deliver my speech, I felt the difference. I was prepared and ready, but I wasn't focused on myself. My attention was on serving my audience. I had their attention, and I knew if I could inspire hope, my speech would be a success. I took Sara's advice and stepped on stage without any paper. The feedback I received proved that having confidence in front of the room and enjoying some fun with your audience creates an impression that is so much stronger than a perfectly written and rehearsed speech.

In this book, Sara takes a deep dive into the many fears of speaking. Her captivating stories make this book easy to digest and difficult to put down. You'll realize that what you have to offer to the world is far more important than any fear that's been holding you back. Sara's thought-provoking perspective and demonstration of what it means to be real make it possible for you to minimize fear and be yourself at the front of the room. Who knows—you might even enjoy it!

Wendi Breuer, CEO/President at SeaChange Print Innovations

Introduction

Visiting my daughter's school takes me back to my elementary school days. *Do all schools smell like this?* I wonder. It's that mix between dirty gym socks and a sparkling, newly scrubbed floor. To me, it smells like learning and makes me smile. My twelve-year-old daughter, Danika, opens the heavy door to the office, now turned music suite. I quickly take a seat. The other moms drop their kids off for voice lessons and go run errands or take the time to chill with a book, sitting in some public space. I never dreamed of missing out; secretly, I've always wanted to sing. As a trainer for public speaking, I am fascinated by the power of the voice, and I love to see the growth that comes from expressing one's self orally.

Dennis, the music teacher, is an opera singer and has performed all over the world. His goofy humor is perfect for a young teenager. He comes alive when he plays the piano. Not because he loves it—he admits he is not a good piano player—but I suspect he loves drawing out the voices from his students' inner beings with his melodic tool. He is old enough to retire, but instead, he chooses to pass on his love of music, for which I am grateful. He uses his hands like a passionate conductor to turn up the volume of

Danika's voice. He encourages her and teaches more than singing.

I learn from him each time I observe his masterful work. You just know he's learned the hard way, as life lessons flow from his mouth—"Fail big because this is the place to do it!"—at just the right time.

When Danika first started taking lessons from him, she worked hard to impress him. She has a beautiful voice and was eager to please. As the weeks passed, I could see her let go of her interest in doing it "right"—she experimented more and started to find her authentic voice.

Sometimes I try to record Danika singing, but when she catches me, she stops. Tonight is one such night. She sounds amazing and I want to capture it. At the end of the piece, Dennis acknowledges her connection with the music, which was last week's lesson. I'm so curious what he will say this time. How could she have done any better?

I always thought voice lessons were more technical and involved hitting notes perfectly. While he pays attention to the technical, his instruction always involves a mind shift or a connection. He knows the voice is an expression of what's going on internally. Gently, he turns to her and says, "When you're singing, be more interested in being understood than in singing."

From that point on, I drift off to a faraway place—you know, the place you go when ideas converge and epiphanies strike. I ponder, *Isn't that what we need to do as speakers? Be more interested in being understood than in speaking? Instead of trying to sound eloquent, articulate, or smart, shouldn't we focus on being understood?*

Doing so would turn our attention to the audience, and we would, in turn, understand them. That is how we connect with our audience. Thank you, Dennis.

Deciding to do what it takes to stand at the front of the room with all those eyes staring back at you is stepping into complete vulnerability, and it takes a lot of courage. This is why speaking will always be a love of mine.

- It has shown me sides of myself I didn't know existed.
- It has shaped me into a leader I never thought I could be.
- It has made me susceptible to the judgment and criticism of others as well as myself.
- It has taught me self-compassion and strengthened my resilience.
- It has forced me to learn my truth and speak it with no apologies.
- It has made me wrestle with the concept of radical self-acceptance, which doesn't require anyone's approval of me.
- It has taught me to STAND TALL.

When I speak to audiences, I feel life course through my veins in a way I've never been able to duplicate. Speaking is living for me, and my hope is that you get to experience speaking in the same way. This book is largely about my internal experience as I've navigated through the many fears of speaking to finally enjoy connecting with audiences from the front of the room. It's also a book of stories from the stage and beyond. My hope is that each story invites you to learn a lesson that spares you pain and discomfort, but more than that, I wish you the courage to take action in spite of your fears.

Chapter 1
THE MANY FEARS OF SPEAKING

"Running away at the height of your anxiety reinforces your fear." – Sara Krisher

Thirty of us piled into a beautiful living-room-type space in a coworking building. It was a Saturday, so the building was empty except for the open space that was reserved for the two-hour class I was taking. People from all walks of life were there. Some I knew, and others I had never met. The fireplace and wood-planked wall made for a cozy place to learn.

Everyone took their seats and our instructor, Jennie, began introducing the topic. She got about five minutes in when a student abruptly pointed at Jennie's legs and said, "Jennie, you have something hanging out of your pants." Everyone turned their attention to Jennie's pants. You could hear a pin drop, and I couldn't, for the life of me, figure out what could be so important about her pants that class had to be interrupted. Jennie was seated with a book in her hands, so she quickly bent over to assess the situation. She was wearing capris with a cuffed hem. She paused for dramatic effect, then suddenly whipped out a dryer sheet and swung it up over her head as she exclaimed, "It's a magic trick! If you think that was impressive, just wait until you see what I have in store for you today." We all chuck-led, and she continued where she left off without skipping a beat.

Jennie took something that could have been extremely embarrassing and had the presence of mind to turn it into something fun. She connected with the audience and made them laugh. No one could have planned it as expertly as it was executed.

Pro Tip

Be prepared: If something embarrassing happens beyond your control. Have the presence of mind to turn it into something funny.

That was authentic confidence. So many of us put extreme amounts of pressure on ourselves to never make a mistake when we present. Confidence at the front of the room is not about being perfect. As much as Jennie had planned and prepared for us to be there, she couldn't have anticipated the scenario that unfolded five minutes in. In her preparation process, when she was thinking about all the things that could go wrong, she would've never thought to herself, *What if a dryer sheet hangs out of my pants and a student interrupts class to point it out? What will I do then?*

Each and every speaking opportunity is therefore a grand experiment. You create a plan, show up, execute the plan, and it works—or it doesn't. In order to be truly confident with what presents itself, you have to be with your audience "in the moment." Your personal power resides in the present, and if you can refrain from thinking about the past or the future, you can fully invest yourself in what is unfolding. You become a part of the experiment, and you can access your wisdom and humor along with all the other attributes that make you an amazing individual.

Harness the Fear

There is no mystery as to why, at all costs, we avoid leading at the front of the room. It can be completely terrifying and anxiety-producing. In fact, early in my career, I personally struggled and squirmed at the mere mention of having to speak to groups.

It's quite unnatural to be placed in front of a group of people with the responsibility of presenting something worthwhile. It's enough to make even the most confident leaders shake in their boots. But being a leader means you must, at some point, stand out or stand up and share with others what direction you're headed in.

Pro Tip

Being a leader means you take the risk to make an impact, and you contribute in the way *only you can* to make a difference.

If you had told me ten years ago that I would be speaking and teaching about the importance of speaking, I would've laughed you out of the room. There wasn't a bone in my body that desired the attention, the judgment, or the responsibility that comes with learning the craft. It's been an adventure full of mishaps, mistakes, and miscalculations. I no longer make predictions about what I will or won't do. I've learned that life will continue to dare me to lean into discomfort.

Pro Tip

The person at the front of the room has not found a way to rid themselves of fear —they have learned how to harness it.

It's easy to think the person at the front of the room has found a way to rid themselves of fear. The truth is that they've learned how to harness it. Speaking to an audience requires bravery, but being brave doesn't mean there is an absence of fear. Being brave means noticing the fear and pushing through it. Once you know what it feels like to act in the face of fear, nerves, and anxiety, it becomes familiar. As you get more familiar with the feelings, you'll no longer see it as a threat, but rather an old friend that shows up to remind you this is something you care about.

Pro Tip

Eventually, the things that take great courage today will no longer require such bravery, and you will become more comfortable.

Showing Up

When I decided to change careers, I deliberately sought out work that would make me a better speaker. Fortunately, I landed a job at a public-speaking training company. I was highly motivated to learn all the technical aspects of delivering a speech because I was under the impression for most of my adult life that there was a right way to speak to audiences. If I were to become a speaker, I had a lot to learn, and I would need to do it flawlessly.

Eventually, my boss handed me a speech she had written and asked me to learn it. It was time for me to begin speaking to audiences, and I needed to be able to demonstrate what I was teaching. I couldn't very well be telling the audience what it takes to be a great speaker if I was going to hide behind a lectern the entire time. The pressure was tremendous, but I was determined. My boss brought a test audience of about nine people together. I would first present to friends and colleagues so I could get valuable feedback for improvement.

All I had to do was learn the speech and deliver it, which was easier said than done. On the day of my fake audience presentation, I did everything I was trained to do. I had great eye contact, I used gestures, I kept my body open and comfortable, I spoke clearly—and I can say without a doubt that I nailed it.

I was shocked when less-than-stellar feedback came back. It seemed my technical skills were on par, but they said that "Sara" didn't show up. I asked them to clarify. Their experience of "Sara" was that I was funny, real, and fun to be with. The presentation was great, *but they didn't get to see me*. At the time, I didn't know what to do with that information. After all, I worked so hard to be what I thought I needed to be, and, in the end, they docked off points for that very skill.

How would I "be Sara" and do this flawlessly? I knew it wasn't possible. If I needed to be funny, real, and fun to be with, I would have to let my guard down, be willing to screw up, be exposed and vulnerable in front of strangers. I couldn't "be Sara" and "be flawless."

Pro Tip

To be successful on stage, you have to let your guard down, and be willing to screw up, be exposed and vulnerable in front of strangers.

Shadow Self

In my coaching studies, I learned about the concept of the shadow self. The shadow self is the side of yourself you keep hidden in places, or at times, you feel it would be inappropriate to show your whole self. Examples include casting aside our sinful ways and refraining from swearing while attending church service, protecting our personal lives while we are at work, so nobody knows we hoard bobblehead dolls, showing up to family gatherings as the middle child—thus our doctorate degrees and recent community awards are not acknowledged, and the list goes on.

I can almost see the shadow self sitting in the corner when a presenter cautiously walks up to the lectern with no emotion and delivers her facts and findings. You may think the audience won't appreciate your full self. The truth is they don't appreciate a dry, uninteresting, robotic presentation. They don't appreciate a person who is unwilling to fully show up.

Pro Tip

Audiences don't appreciate a dry, uninteresting, robotic presentation—or a person who is unwilling to fully show up.

What I held back is what the audience wanted to see. What I protected was what I needed to set free. What I feared is what I needed to step into. My full self, flawed as I am, was being called forth to lead. My whole self was being beckoned to express itself.

This is the ultimate journey to the front of the room. It's not about what you say or do, how charismatic you are, or how you put words together so eloquently. It's giving yourself permission to show up fully and be seen in a way you've never been seen before.

You see, what makes you so smart is also what makes you funny. What makes you approachable is what makes you trustworthy. What makes you credible is what makes you curious. Embracing your shadow self means you will be able to experience freedom at the front of the room. It also means you will be able to hear your greatest fears. And in those fears, you will hear your heart's desires. You will awaken to the voice that you've been hearing faint whispers from all these years but couldn't make out the words. You will live fully. You will know what joy means. You will know vitality.

Chapter 2
FEAR OF CRITICISM

"Strive to make a connection because perfection is not relatable or attainable."– Sara Krisher

The swipe of the windshield wipers was mesmerizing. Back and forth, back and forth, with a little thump at the end of each pass. It was bright outside, and the roads were covered with melting snow. Nothing was falling from the sky, but the spray from the cars in front of me made it impossible to see without a constant squirt of fluid and a few swipes from the wipers. It had been three hours since I had left after having a great visit with Mom. I was halfway home from the small town in northern Wisconsin, where she lived. I was only nineteen years old, so my crappy car and the few dollars I had to my name prevented me from visiting as often as I'd liked.

The drive home that day would forever be imprinted in my memory. In fact, you might even say it changed the trajectory of my life. The past three hours had been uneventful until this point in the journey—so uneventful, I found it hard to keep my eyes open. The road put me in a narcoleptic trance, and I did one of those quick head bobs. You know, the kind where you think you may have actually fallen asleep in the half-second your eyes shut. I glanced up, and to my horror, a school bus was headed straight toward me. I had drifted into oncoming traffic! I yanked the steering wheel and swerved back into my lane.

I'm awake now! I thought to myself. I pulled into the next gas station to refresh myself. I didn't need gas but decided to top off the tank while I check my windshield wiper fluid and the oil level in my car. My dad would be proud. I took my time cleaning off each window and headed in to use the bathroom, where I did twenty-five jumping jacks to get some blood moving in my body. Feeling good about my energy level, I grabbed a snack and paid for my gas. The clerk followed me out of the store to shovel the walk.

Feeling responsible and confident, I hopped back in the car and drove off. But something wasn't right. No, something was definitely not right. I didn't get more than ten feet away, and my car jolted. I hadn't ever felt this before, so I wasn't sure what to make of it. Just then, I looked to my left, and I saw the store clerk fling her shovel to the ground and hightail it into the store. Now I was really worried. Had I run over a small animal, or a worse, maybe a child? It felt like I hit a pothole. That seemed a likely scenario because I hadn't seen anything in front of me. As I glanced forward, I saw motion in my rearview mirror. Disbelief filled my head while billowing flames reaching thirty feet into the sky danced erratically just behind my car. I froze. I heard someone yell, "Get out of the car!" To this day, I don't know if that was a guardian angel or a real person because nobody was around. I followed orders. I jumped out of my car, looked behind me, and in an instant, I understood what had happened. The gas pump nozzle was still connected to my car! I never pulled it out and set it back in its cradle. It was one of those old gas stations without an overhead canopy. When I drove off, the entire gas tank broke from its platform, which explains the sudden jolt, and I dragged it about six feet. The fast-acting clerk had run inside to hit the emergency shut-off button. This was all my fault! I had caused all this. Soon after, the fire department came, the police came, and the store manager had to close the place down. It was a disaster.

All I could think was that I barely had enough money to cover the gas I put in my tank. Were they going to charge me for the gas I blew up? Maybe they would throw me in jail for destruction of property. The police officer approached me and took my statement. I was sobbing as he asked me if I could call someone to pick me up. I was three hours from home and three hours from my mom. Nobody was going to come to my rescue. He suggested in a really careful voice that I go across the street to the Hardees and have a cup of coffee. *How absurd,* I thought. *I don't want to hang out in the town I just destroyed. Plus, I've got three hours of driving left and I'm wide awake now!* As an adult, I can appreciate the suggestion of a bit of downtime to gather my wits before venturing on, so off I went.

I spent the next three hours of my life reflecting on how untrustworthy, irresponsible, and ashamed I was for having caused so much damage. I contemplated how close

I came to accidentally killing someone. I considered how close I came to having blown up the entire block if the quick-thinking clerk had not been on her game. I wondered if my insurance company would catch on to the fact that I was high-risk and didn't deserve to be insured. I felt a great amount of remorse for what I did and for what I almost did. I didn't tell Mom for two years. She wondered why I kept bringing random friends to her house from that point on. I couldn't pump my own gas for weeks. Even now when I pump gas, I have a heightened sense of my surroundings. Time slows down, and I am hyperalert, noticing each move I make. I check the pump over and over before driving off. I replay it unwittingly like a reoccurring nightmare.

I never paid for the gas I blew up or the damages to the station, but I did pay dearly for that mistake. I dug a deep groove in my psyche that day and poured in a belief that I was unintentionally bad. I consider that worse than being a bad person. At least if you are a bad person, you are choosing to be bad, and you know it. I considered myself to be a bad person, but merely by accident. I was accidentally bad, and who knows what kind of future danger was in store. I was a disaster.

The experience brought me wisdom I couldn't have pulled from a bookshelf. But if I had read the lesson, it would go something like this: Life is full of accidental screw-ups. Some are bigger than others. When you're tired of punishing yourself and collecting stories of inadequacy, make a decision to forgive yourself. Forgiveness is not a feeling, nor is it an admission that what happened doesn't matter. It's a decision. Holding onto the shame and beating yourself up only makes you suffer. It's not productive.

Pro Tip

Stop punishing yourself and collecting stories of inadequacy—and decide to forgive yourself. Forgiveness is not a feeling nor is it an admission that what happened doesn't matter.

Offer yourself the same grace you would a dear friend. Separate yourself from the problem and make meaning of the lesson so you can live a life you love.

♦ ♦ ♦ ♦ ♦

Speaker's Input:

I teach coaching skills to adults, and I had just completed setting up my room for the new students that would be coming to class. It's so important to make a good first impression, so I displayed my materials beautifully for each one of them, made sure the chairs were in an inviting circle formation and opened the windows for some fresh outdoor breeze.

Never in a million years did I think opening the windows would have had such a profound effect on me. I didn't consider that it was hay fever season, and my allergies would send me into a sneezing attack. I wore light-colored linen pants, and with one last sneeze, I peed my pants! All of the students had just arrived and witnessed it all.

There was no hiding the fact that I just humiliated myself. I did my best to make light of my untimely mishap and explained that no matter how much they fail in class this semester, it will never be as traumatic as peeing yourself in front of all your pupils.

That day it was me who became the student—and the experience became my teacher.

Jennie Antolak, President at Learning Journeys International Center of Coaching

◆◆◆◆◆

Journey to Oneself—Finding "Home"

As a TED Talk filled my earbuds with the voice of author Elizabeth Gilbert, I was introduced to the concept of coming home. She spoke of the overwhelming success she experienced after publishing her book, *Eat, Pray,*

Love, and how it felt as if nothing would ever top that or compete with it. She felt there was no place to go, and she knew any writing she did after that would be scrutinized and most assuredly fail. It haunted her, and she couldn't see her way past it. She found herself searching for a safe place to find herself again. For her, it was her writing that took her "home" to herself. She spoke of her writing being her retreat. It was where she reconnected with herself—and that's what moved her forward from the hopeless place she was stuck.

I stumbled on this concept again reading Sara Bareilles's book *It Sounds Like Me.* She is a musician, singer, and songwriter. She shares in her book her year-long study abroad and how utterly lonely and lost she felt at one point. Sara fell to her knees and asked God to show her a place that resembled home. Soon after, she called her dad in desperation, sobbing and pleading with him to send her keyboard. It didn't occur to her until then that home meant writing and singing, and that's what she needed to do to come back to herself.

We leave home when we are young adults and venture into the world to make a space for ourselves. For some of us, it takes years to learn that all we're really searching for is a place to call home. I find myself wondering if that's what's wrong with the world today. Maybe we are all just looking for a place to call home—a place we can retreat to when we are disconnected from ourselves. Only we don't realize it, and we ping pong from place to place only getting further from who we are meant to be. Some never find it.

Some are destined to know from an early age, and the lucky ones can recognize it despite outside pressures.

Home is a place inside of one's self, protected from the pressures of expectation. It's a place you go to feel safe, accepted, and complete. It's a soft space absent the judgment of self and others. It's where you go when you need to be still and steady yourself from despair, ridicule, and abandonment. It's a place to be vulnerable and notice what is. Blame and guilt don't live in the quiet, restful retreat. Home is where you soak in the warmth of now and cleanse the need to choose or be indecisive. Home is where peace wraps around you, soothing your soul while you sit still. It's where you can fully breathe in and out. You can show up as you are, scars and all. You can visit as much as you like, and you leave feeling ready and strong.

Each of us has a place to call home, but we aren't always open to its invitation. It comes to us in our dark moments. It whispers to us when we're alone. We have to be willing to go to it.

Pro Tip

Explore and find what feels like home to you. It's there that you will be your truest self.

"Presentation Lacked Substance"

Those words were written feedback I received after a presentation. The gut-punch took my breath away. The other great sentiments only tiptoed on the page. Their light and encouraging words hopped away to make room for the other words stomping my self-esteem. Of all the feedback I could get, this one was the most hurtful!

Pro Tip

The fear of criticism is a fear of not being worthy or enough."

I didn't understand how this could have been, so I got angry. I was mad there wasn't more information. I was frustrated someone would write this about the presentation I had put so much heart into. I was irritated I couldn't ask clarifying questions. I was curious if others felt the same. My brain replayed the three-hour workshop on a loop. Yes, I could've done better. Yes, I wasn't perfect. What I didn't understand was how the owner of these words hadn't been affected by any of the content, the delivery, or the experience—I had failed.

Those three words had me spiraling down into one of the most dreaded fears in public speaking: the fear of criticism. If I could pull back the fear of criticism's mask, I believe we'd see a fear of not being worthy or not being enough. It's in our nature to want to belong. It used to be a survival instinct. If we didn't run in a tribe, we would succumb to the elements and die. Of course, now there's Amazon Prime, but we still have an innate need to belong.

The words cut deep because they confirmed my fear of not belonging. Standing in front of an audience requires me to courageously open myself up, be vulnerable, and show up authentically so they can truly see me. It's the best way to approach the stage, my audience, and quite frankly—life. I don't claim to be perfect, and I definitely make mistakes. I know I can always do better. Every piece of criticism has the potential to hit me hard because I let my squishy center show. As a result, they're not just criticizing my speech; they're criticizing my being.

Pro Tip

Show up authentically so they can truly see you—it's the best way to approach the stage, your audience, and quite frankly—life.

The overachiever in me kicks my inner critic into high gear before and after a speech. I do not need criticism from others to do better. I do my absolute best each time I show up. That being said, I know I cannot rid the world of criticism, so I have learned to deal with it.

Ten Ideas to Overcome Harsh Criticism:

1. If you have not asked for the feedback, you don't have to accept it. The best feedback always comes from a trusted source and is something you ask for and can receive.
2. If you can't discern what the feedback means, disregard it. If it is not specific or constructive, it is not helpful.
3. Get some sleep and let some time pass. All criticism gets less sharp as time goes on.
4. The feedback might not even be about you. The person giving you the criticism may be going through something, and you just happen to intersect with him or her at an inconvenient moment.
5. Call a supportive friend and really hear what they have to say. Write down the positive comments you receive.
6. Your time on stage is not about you—it's about what happens because of you. Know that you have value with those that are ready to receive, and that may not be everyone.
7. Read your positive feedback and believe it. Don't dismiss it.
8. Adopt a growth mindset. You're always improving, so take what is valuable. Anything else is irrelevant.
9. Extend yourself the same compassion you would your best friend. Be good to you.

10. Take on Brené Brown's perspective: "If you're not in the arena also getting your ass kicked, I'm not interested in your feedback."

The fear of criticism can have us scrambling to fit in. When we take the stage, however, we are standing out. The stage is about radical acceptance of self and others, and that takes incredible courage.

My sincere advice: STAND TALL in the way only you can. The world needs more *you*.

Chapter 3
FEAR OF NOT KNOWING ENOUGH

"How you are BEING speaks louder than words."
– Sara Krisher

My first speech out of the country was in Warsaw, Poland. In the month leading up to the trip, I did the best I could to prepare myself. I overpacked a large suitcase and a carry-on. I had the adapter for my hairdryer and phone. I called my credit card companies to let them know I would be in Poland. I had music, audiobooks, magazines, and a book to keep me busy on the long flight. I even downloaded an app to learn Polish.

I stepped onto the plane that day feeling as prepared as I could for this trip across the Atlantic. I'll describe myself as *cautiously confident*. However, stepping foot on foreign ground just a few hours later was a shock to my system. I panicked when I was no longer able to read words or symbols plastered all over the airport walls. I was no longer able to make out what was being said. I felt completely disoriented and didn't feel prepared at all. Somehow, I was able to get into a taxi and get to my hotel, but even spending money was confusing. Everything I took for granted every day was absent. My anxiety was off the charts, and I felt completely vulnerable. I told myself I would never do this again. I would never put myself in such an incredibly uncomfortable position ever again.

That may have been the first time I've traveled out of the United States, but it wasn't the first time I felt completely vulnerable, exposed, and unprepared after being confident I was ready. I have, on many occasions, felt ready and confident enough to give a speech, but looking out at the audience took my breath away, and not in a good way.

I often hear that practice is the antidote to this anxiety—to which I say, "Bologna!" I'm not implying that preparation is futile. Instead, I'd like to shine a big bright, bold light on "the right preparation is key." After many years of panic and terror during speaking experiences like this, I've learned a few things.

Here are three truths to consider for yourself:

1. Everyone has their own unique preparation process for speaking. (They may not have discovered it yet.)
2. Practice does not make perfect—in this case, experience is key, and there is no "perfect." (Experience, experience, experience; there is no substitute for the real deal.)
3. Preparing your body is just as important as preparing your mind. (Be ready with strategies to calm yourself in the heat of the moment.)

I said earlier that I would never travel outside the U.S. again, but the truth is, I have and will again. I met incredible people who became my good friends. I was introduced to a land with unimaginable history. I witnessed the amazing architecture standing tall where ruins once blanketed the landscape. I left Warsaw, Poland, with gratitude. The discomfort and anxiety at the beginning of my trip gave way to curiosity and confidence. This is exactly how I've experienced my speaking journey, too. Every speaking opportunity can be both terrifying and gratifying. Every presentation is a chance to discover who I am and what I'm capable of. All of the anxiety and discomfort become worth it because the payoff is the chance to make a difference in life. If you could make a difference in one person's life with your presentation, would it be worth it to you?

Pro Tip

All of the anxiety and discomfort become worth it because the payoff is the chance to make a difference—in even one person's life.

When I first began speaking, I didn't feel qualified to make any difference. I mean, who was I to think I could make an impact in another's life? I wasn't sure who I was supposed to be talking to or what I should be saying.

Unfortunately, the fear of not knowing enough becomes the reason many don't make it to the front of the room. Instead of speaking to an audience, they stay safe, and thus they forfeit leadership, stunt potential, and reject opportunity. So how do you know if you know enough?

You'll know you're ready to connect with your audience if you can go six questions deep.

The following six questions are key to providing some assurance that you do know your subject matter, and you will be ready to share your message.

1. **What is the purpose in sharing your message?**
    Your purpose will align your thoughts, actions, and message, which will ultimately assist in accomplishing what you set out to do. How does your purpose serve your audience?

2. **What does your audience need to know?**
    This is the critical point, and it's best if it's short and sweet. Imagine your audience reflecting on your presentation two weeks later. What do they need to remember?

3. **What makes this message so important to you as the speaker?**
    Make a personal connection with your material. Ultimately, if you aren't connected to your material, your audience won't be either. When

your audience understands why the message is important to you, they can more easily trust you and your motives.

4. **What evidence do you have to support your thoughts, ideas, and assumptions?**
A good rule of thumb is to come up with three points you want to make to support your critical point, and use your evidence to bolster those three points. What can you share that is relevant to your audience?

5. **What is your commitment to the topic or message?**
You've been asked to share the message because you are deemed the appropriate one based on your background. Leverage your experience as well as your knowledge. Your worst practices, mistakes, and slipups have value and make you relatable, so don't be afraid to share the good, the bad, and the ugly.

6. **How will you ensure that your message extends beyond this initial communication?**
Find a way for your audience to integrate their learning with their life, their work, or their process, and make it last after their time with you is over. What tools, methods, and shortcuts can you equip them with to assist them in their life?

Tacit Knowledge

You've been asked to deliver a message not only because you are knowledgeable but because you have a unique set of experiences that contribute to a distinct perspective. You are in possession of tacit knowledge, which is difficult to pass along to others. Think about the difference between knowing how to ride a bike and being able to teach someone how to ride a bike. If all your audience wanted was explicit knowledge, they would've asked you to write a manual, share a technical diagram, or they would've found the information online and skipped inviting you to speak. What you know and how you explain it are fundamentally what makes you so qualified to share. Maybe they've heard a similar message from four other people, but the way you explained it, at the time you explained it, made it stick.

Pro Tip

What you know and how you explain it are fundamentally what makes you so qualified to share.

◆◆◆◆◆

Speaker's Input:

I was asked to fly to Germany and present to a group of high-level executives from a large corporation, and I was so nervous I prepped the PowerPoint for weeks. Part of what I thought would calm me down was choosing the perfect outfit. I had hoped that the ritual of putting on clothes and makeup that made me feel confident would help me be confident during the presentation. I was losing sleep and got more and more nervous as the flight date approached. I even tried unsuccessfully to get out of going on the trip.

The day came and I finally arrived, and the long flight was well, long. I was traveling in a small group, and when we got to the baggage claim in the Munich airport, everyone was able to claim their luggage except for me because mine was somewhere else. My presentation was early the next morning, and I was hoping that they would find it, but nope! Two other women made the trip from Silicon Valley, and one of them graciously offered to loan me an outfit.

I cannot exactly remember what it was, but it ended with khaki pants. This was not exactly the look I was going for. To make matters worse, I was fairly thin and felt that the pants were going to fall off. I felt bad after asking the woman for a belt as it seemed like she had taken it a little personally. I was the third person to present. I remember getting up there and telling the story of what had happened to the suitcase, and the Germans in the audience seemed to get a good chuckle out of my story. That helped me become more confident as I launched into my PowerPoint.

What I learned from that experience is you should always pack a carry-on with your most important items when you travel on an airplane. The second thing I learned is that the ability to laugh at yourself goes a long way in helping your audience relate to you and trust you rather quickly.

Kristin Wermus, Master-Certified Coach, Level 1 Coaching Facilitator at Learning Journeys International School of Coaching

◆◆◆◆◆

What You Believe about Your Audience Matters

I had a fundamental belief that salespeople were dishonest and always tried to trick their prospects into buying. I thought they were out to serve their needs and could care less about the collateral damage they caused. I thought they made all of the money and didn't do any of the work.

So, when I became a salesperson, I just knew I would be a rock star. I was going to do circles around all of these incompetent, sleazy, unfocused salespeople with bad work ethics that weren't respected by anyone. I worked really hard for the next few years. Bosses told me I had so much potential—but I wasn't reaching it. Not even close.

One day in speaking with the owner of the company, I explained my frustration. And like most owners, she was too busy running the business to help, so she hired me a coach. Being at my wits' end, I was open to the idea. I mean, if a coach could see something I wasn't doing correctly, then hallelujah! I was certain that she wouldn't find anything. I mean I was hard-working, dedicated, personable, and I knew my stuff! Bring it on, coach! Session one was painful. I didn't realize I was going to be asked questions that made me squirm, made me think, and made me want to run out the door. Most of the questions I didn't know the answer to. I was in my mid-twenties. What did I know about life and what I valued? What exactly were values? It wasn't until the second session that we uncovered something. Eureka! I actually hated being called a salesperson. I didn't like the stigma it carried. How could I identify myself as a sleazy, unfocused, lazy salesperson? Suddenly, I saw my problem. How could I be the very thing I hated? I rejected the notion of identifying with the title so much so that I was ineffective in my work. I didn't hand off work to the designers because I thought I could do it and earn their respect. I didn't ask for the sale, but in an attempt to be "non-salesy," I would do everything I could for the client to earn their respect.

In the end, I was spending too much time doing "non-salesy" activities and tiptoed around any discussions about the "price." It was so clear to me then. I had a restricting belief that held me back from being successful. I needed to redefine what it meant to be a salesperson in a positive way so I could fully embrace the role. When I looked closer, I could see that good salespeople were consultants with a service mindset and brilliant negotiating skills, who could handle tough conversations and resolve conflict with ease.

Within a year, I was the top saleswoman in the company. I was bringing in $2.5 million in sales and making an amount of money I didn't think I would ever make. I let the designers do their job. I delegated where possible. I displayed a positive attitude because I was having a blast.

Pro Tip

Each of us has a belief system that we've cultivated through experience. Usually, the belief is formed without our even knowing it.

I still don't know where I formed the belief that sales-people are sleazy. Maybe it was a television show or a movie that depicted them poorly, or maybe I encountered some sleazy salespeople in my life.

We form beliefs about our job abilities, our health, our relationships with significant others, money, the list goes on. We shape our reality with these beliefs until everything we look at is filtered through the lens we created. These filters are why two people can witness the same situation and have completely different conclusions. Some were formed at a very young age from listening to our parents. Some we pick up along life's journey.

We don't stop to take the time to reevaluate our thinking until we realize our current thought process is not working. Not all of our beliefs are bad, however. We are able to protect ourselves from inherent danger because we've formed healthy beliefs. A healthy or positive belief is one that serves you. For example, if you get burned by a hot stove once, the next time you avoid going near the stove entirely because you believe you will get burned. This is the way our mind protects us from danger.

Pro Tip

Beliefs are revealed with our words, so don't skip having thoughtful contemplation regarding your beliefs about your audience.

In my current work, I ready leaders for speaking. I imagine I am the audience and listen from that perspective. I can spot instantly when the speaker's belief about the audience is not favorable. You can't come from an adversary position and expect you will get them on board. You've got to invite them along with you, to imagine, and to trust you, so you've got to be on their side.

I was so excited to take a class from a highly respected speaker. She was well known, and her class was top dollar. A few minutes in, I felt like I was being scolded for my lack of knowledge and for my ineptness. I got the impression she thought everyone in the audience was dumb. Maybe it was a tactic to get people to understand how smart and capable she was and how we ought to hire her for consulting. It wasn't effective or appreciated by me. Had I worked with her, I would have encouraged her to be more relatable by sharing her knowledge and not spend her time saving us from our status as idiots.

◆◆◆◆◆

Speaker's Input:

One morning, I was delivering a half-day presentation to high-level sales profess-sionals. After the first 30 minutes, I hit my groove and felt good about how things were going. I had a good deal of space on the stage and was conscious about involving everyone in the room by moving from one side to another while making my points. It wasn't my first rodeo, as I had been speaking to audiences for years.

My goal was to inspire growth and change and have it continue long after my absence. Everything I did was focused on the salespeople's confidence so they could change their behavior when they left the room. If they didn't build confidence, they would not apply the content I shared.

As I moved across the stage, I could see their heads follow me in unison. I started using voice inflections. The softer I spoke, the more they leaned in; the louder I was, the more they leaned back. Some were not taking notes. My first reaction was that they weren't listening, but their head movement told me they were picking up what I was putting down. I realized that the audience was paying attention. I thought, *This is what people look like when they are watching a movie.* They were hanging on my every word and watching my every movement.

I almost interpreted their expressionless demeanor incorrectly. I've learned that the audience may not always look like you think they should, but that doesn't mean they aren't listening and taking it all in.

Scott Plum, President/Founder of Minnesota Sales Institute, LLC

♦♦♦♦♦

Chapter 4
FEAR OF THE UNKNOWN

"How will you ever know what's possible if you don't take the leap?" – Sara Krisher

That itchy restlessness creeps into your mind and slowly wraps around your body until you need to move. You wiggle and twitch, but that's not enough. You know a bold move is required. The problem is you aren't sure where you are going. How will you ever make a confident move if you aren't sure what you want and what the next step should be? The only thing you are sure of is that sitting still isn't working. Staying put is becoming more uncomfortable than making a change. You're trapped, but you still realize you have choice. The choice is what paralyzes you. So, you pause again. This is tension. It's neither good nor bad, and yet it's extremely uncomfortable. Tension is intuition's way of alerting our minds and bodies that change is needed. It's the soul's way of speaking up. Often tension slithers in when you should be happy. You have everything you worked hard for, and you have no huge complaints. You can't point to a single broken or convincing reason to make a move. Many people would be elated with the life you've built. Your mind says,

"It's not that bad. I have a lot of reasons to be grateful, and I'd be a fool to make a move when all is going well."

This is Tension

I sat across from a woman who was looking for a life coach, one of a few coaches she would be meeting with before deciding who was the best fit. I asked her one of the first questions anyone in my position might ask: "What makes you interested in coaching?" She looked back at me with desperate eyes and said she didn't know exactly. She went on to explain how she had been feeling. She stumbled over her words as if this were the first time she was untangling what she already knew. She shared with me when it started and how it wouldn't go away. She was looking for answers to a question that hadn't been formed yet. *This is tension.*

Tension makes us seek. In the quiet moments, tension confronts us like a nagging child. Those that choose to listen are the ones that dare to do more. They hear the calling. They don't judge; they merely listen. Tension doesn't go away. It can be snuffed out with busyness. It can be avoided with blame and irritability. If ignored, it shows up as frustration, disappointment, regret, anger, and sadness. The cost is great. These feelings will flow through your body like a poison until everything you do is a restricted effort that's shadowed by fear. The swirling mess of negativity will make it nearly impossible for you to hear what you are meant to do.

Tension is a feeling. It shows up and gets stronger over time. It creates a divide between *what is* and *what must be.* It's what leads a doctor to pack up, leave a successful practice, and move to Missouri to run a llama farm. It's what makes a high-powered attorney quit working so much—and give some of his time to charity. It's the internal nudge you get that tells you when change is necessary. When you recognize it for what it is and listen to what it calls you to do, amazing exploration will ensue. Your life is meant to be rich, full, and lived. Your soul knows that. Let your mind and body follow.

Tension is what I felt before I left my 16-year career in business-to-business sales to begin a new career in speaking, training, and coaching. I put up with the tension for years. I wondered, *What if?* and dreamed about what my life could be. I heard people throw the word *potential* around, but to me, it was a mirage. Just when I thought I could envision my future, it would fade out of sight, and I'd be left wondering if what I saw was real. I yearned to give back and make an impact in the world. The nudge never went away, and I ended up getting physically ill. Doctors couldn't find anything wrong with me. When I made the decision to pursue my dreams and backed it up with action, my physical symptoms vanished.

I still feel tension, but it's more like a tap on the shoulder than a kick in the pants. I don't question it as much. I trust the tension to give me direction, but I never get the full picture of how it will all work out. That's where faith in something larger than yourself comes in handy.

Pro Tip

**Your life is meant to be rich,
full, and lived.**

Speaking is Dynamic

My boss delivered the news to me with enthusiasm: "You're scheduled to speak at the upcoming conference for business leaders, and there will be two hundred in attendance!" I was working at a public-speaking training company—and the stakes could not be higher. My boss, peers, and potential clients would be watching what would unfold. I would be speaking about the top five most important elements of a great presentation, and I'd need to demonstrate them flawlessly. My credibility was on the line. The lump in my throat was the size of a grapefruit.

It was not a new speech. In fact, I had presented the speech about twenty times already. The difference was that I had presented it to groups of twenty or less. I became familiar with how that looked and how I would "be" in that type of environment. I felt comfortable.

This was completely different—at least it felt that way. The idea of speaking to two hundred people was overwhelming. It might as well have been two thousand people. My safety net split. Nothing about it seemed familiar, and none of my previous experience put me at ease. I recognize this now as the fear of the unknown.

I didn't know how I would "be" in front of two hundred people.

- What would it feel like?
- Would I be able to do all of the same things I could do in front of twenty?
- Would they appreciate my attempts to engage them?
- Would I need to speak louder? Move more?
- Would I remember what I needed to say with all this pressure?

It all felt like a huge risk.

I knew it was a good speech because it was a hit with those that heard me give it on many previous occasions. I knew the material and the PowerPoint so well that I could do it at the drop of a hat. My boss had faith in me, and I trusted her judgment. It was still nerve-wracking for me because this would be the very first time in front of this particular audience, sharing this content in this space and time. In that way, it was all new and largely unknown. Not being able to recognize anything as familiar is a uniquely terrifying experience.

We draw on what we know in order to anticipate experiences, and it informs us how we feel about them. The problem is the only experience you might have to draw on is the embarrassment you faced in school, the agony of a failed client presentation, or the sheer panic of having to present to an executive. If you haven't replaced those few memories with more supportive and empowering experiences, it's difficult to imagine anything else. You may need to channel the success that you've had in other areas of your life.

When the day came to present, I looked out at the audience, took a deep breath, and started. The response from the crowd was familiar, like I had been there before.

♦♦♦♦♦

Speaker's Input:

One of my most embarrassing moments happened to be one of my very first speeches. I was only ten years old, living in a small town in Iowa. Everyone in my class had to give a speech. I was excited because I thought it would be easy and fun. I'm naturally outgoing and love to speak to groups, even back then. When the teacher asked for a volunteer, my hand shot up. I don't remember the topic I was presenting, but I got to go first.

As I started to read from my paper and look up and down like we were taught, a loud noise interrupted me. I was just as surprised as everyone else, and I could feel my face get red hot as I realized what had happened. That loud noise came from me! Undeniably, it was a fart. Time stood still, and I had nowhere to hide. My classmates were dying with laughter while I was dying of humiliation. I don't even remember finishing my speech.

Thankfully, it didn't hold me back from getting to the front of the room again. I've given many speeches since that day, and I've learned to clench my butt cheeks to prevent loud noises. For me, success in delivering a speech is *anytime I don't humiliate myself!*

**—Amy Davis, Founder of
Shore Up, LLC**

♦♦♦♦♦

We draw on these memories as we look at the impending doom we face. Years may have passed and knowledge gained, and still, we end up feeling like we have no idea what to expect. The common inclination with speaking is to memorize a script or cling tightly to a PowerPoint deck to control everything within our power. Basically, we try to lock down everything possible to ensure there are no surprises.

But surprise! Speaking is not static—it's dynamic. That's what makes it so challenging and rewarding. It's better to expect the unexpected than to assume you can control all the details. I like to say it's not if but when something shows up that you hadn't planned—the audio-visual equipment not working, the microphone not turning on, lights in your face so you can't see anyone, or your contact saying your speech needs to be cut in half five minutes before you speak.

Pro Tip

**Speaking is dynamic so
expect the unexpected.**

Keep in mind your character is always on display. No matter what happens, your job is to roll with the punches, be gracious, and remember that it's a privilege to speak. You have the time and attention of an audience—and that is an absolute treasure.

♦♦♦♦♦

Speaker's Input:

I was speaking to about 150 attorneys, CPAs, trust advisors, and high-wealth financial planners in Knoxville, Tennessee, when the bulb blew on the projector. No problem. I had a hard copy of the Power-Point and so did the audience. Once the bulb was replaced by a technician, I continued. Then, the projector got hot, started smoking, and it died. We unplugged the projector, and I went on. Shortly after that, the only available microphone died.

I then walked to the center of the group and stood in the middle of the audience. There, I kept slowly turning 360 degrees, speaking with a booming voice so the audience could hear. On the evaluations, I received a 4.9 out of a 5.0. By staying cool even under pressure, they really bonded with me, felt the uncomfortableness, and I believe felt great that the presentation simply continued. I think they actually bonded much better with me without the PowerPoint slides and microphone. It ended up being one of my favorite days ever. The evaluation I received was one of my best ever from a client, and I use it with my speaker page.

Michael A. Gregory, Consultant, Speaker, and Author at Michael Gregory Consulting, LLC

♦♦♦♦♦

You name it, it can happen. That is not meant to scare you, but rather open your eyes to the realities. No amount of control can keep you flexible, at ease, and full of grace in these situations. Prepare the best you can in advance, but be present as soon as you step out of the car in the parking lot.

Pro Tip

Be willing to work with what shows up and laugh at yourself. We are all human.

How to Refocus Your Thoughts for Confidence

- Dwell on the evidence you have that it could go well. If you focus on it, you will find what you are looking for.
- Let curiosity guide you in being flexible and open. You'll be present and able to access your personal power.
- Prepare in a way that supports and empowers you. Writing a script may not be building your confidence. Find what does.
- Focus on your audience and how you can serve them. When your attention is on them, it's not about you, but rather what they need from you.

Pro Tip

**The next time you are asked to speak,
channel your strength.**

You have likely communicated successfully to others and not given yourself any credit. Draw on those experiences. If you truly can't think of a scenario, then pull from something difficult you've overcome in your life. What fueled you? What did you do to rise up and face it? How can you channel that strength now? If you are still struggling to find the champion inside you, be still. Your calm mind will gladly take you to the place you find your strength.

Chapter 5
FeaR OF FaILURe

"Your inner critic speaks the loudest when you step out of your comfort zone." – Sara Krisher

Tiptoeing across the ancient cobblestone sidewalk in my pumps was like walking a high wire, knowing one slip would be the end of me. I was on my way to deliver a presentation in Prague and had been eagerly anticipating it for nine months.

When the call for proposals came out for speaking at a coaching conference in the Czech Republic, I knew I was meant to be there. A month previous, over the holidays, Mom had shared with me that the one place she'd like to visit most in the whole world was the Czech Republic. We have ancestors there, and Mom wanted to see where our family came from all those years ago. I don't believe in coincidences. I believe in connections. I believe there are reasons and opportunities, and if we look closely, we can connect the dots to find meaning. This was meant to be.

Mom and I flew to Prague a few days early so we could tour the awe-inspiring city. The architecture and sculptures were so unreal I could have easily mistaken them for a carefully crafted backdrop of a romantic movie set back in the 1600s.

I bought a new dress for the speech. When I asked how many people I could expect in the audience, I was told anywhere from fifty to two hundred. So, I printed two hundred handouts and planned for two hundred attentive faces. I figured I better err on the side of a big crowd so I would be ready for anything. What a privilege it would be to present to coaches from all over the world. My speech was titled "Public Speaking: The New Public Connecting." It was about how to connect with your audience.

The Uber driver held the car door open for my mom and me as we wedged ourselves in the back of the tiny European car on the way to the conference center. The only way I could fit my 6'1" body in the back seat was to crouch and turn sideways so I had someplace to put my legs. It was only a fifteen-minute drive, so I didn't buckle up.

I was hyperaware that I would be speaking soon, and anxiety was kicking in. My mind was flooded with "what if" questions. *What if I forget what to say? What if they don't like what I have to say? What if I screw up or offend someone?* I couldn't get full breaths. It was not a new feeling—and I fully expected it to show up. I started running through my confidence boosters, deep breaths, stretching (which was impossible in that car), and repeating a mantra in my head. *I got this. I got this. I got this.* I think Mom was trying to distract me by talking about our trip.

Just then, our driver slammed on his brakes. A car had swerved in front of him, and he reacted instantly, thank God. Mom's knees rammed the back of the front passenger seat while my head struck the roof of the car. The driver couldn't speak English, but I could tell he felt terrible and was trying to find out if we were okay.

I was stunned. I understood what had happened, but I wasn't certain I was okay. My head was on fire. In a strange cosmic way, I felt like I was thumped on my head. The sensation made me think I was bleeding. That would be a first—presenting with blood dripping down my face. Wouldn't that get the audience's attention? No blood was visible, and I tried to regain some sort of composure before walking into the conference center. I didn't know whether I should be mad, scared, or sad. How do you react when the universe thumps you on the head?

What does it mean, I thought? *What am I supposed to learn from this?* I wondered if I was supposed to be paying attention to something. It couldn't be for nothing. The timing and the experience were just too perfectly situated right before a really important presentation about connections.

The thump must have knocked some sense into me because my anxiety vanished, and I was so grateful we didn't get into a collision—that could have been our last breath. Mom could've badly hurt her knees. She'd had two knee replacements already. I became so grateful I was alive and could put words together. How I delivered my speech became insignificant.

Five minutes before I went live, only twenty people were in my audience. The room was big enough to accommodate at least three hundred people. They trickled in slow enough that I could greet each person with a handshake and acknowledge them by name. I made sure to glance at their nametag before locking eyes with them and attempting to pronounce their name. I smiled graciously and asked each of them to sit on one side of the room. There was a huge stage, but I wouldn't be using it today. Instead, I talked with them from the floor level. They were very interactive and easy to chat with. I ended up with a total of thirty-eight coaches from all over the world in my audience. At the end of the presentation on connecting, I asked what one thing they would remember about the speech. Person after person remarked at how special they felt when they walked into the room. They mentioned how I pronounced their names, made eye contact, smiled, shook their hands. They appreciated me standing at floor level. At one point, I wondered if I even needed to present at all. It seemed the most impactful part of my presentation was when they walked into the room. It wasn't the research, talking points, or well-crafted supporting stories that brought the importance home.

Pro Tip

Demonstrating what connection looks and feels like is important. We all crave connection.

We can't know what someone in our audience will take away from our presence at the front of the room. We can only do our best to serve the brilliant people before us. I believe the significant thump on my head was a wake-up call. A higher power wanted me to stop obsessing about myself and my performance, and recalibrate to be a present-minded connector. Being grateful for being alive is certainly one way to become present to what is in front of you.

How to Recalibrate in the Moment without a Thump on the Head

- Be in service to your audience.
- Release control of the outcome.
- Be curious.
- Work with what shows up.
- Let go of doing it "right."

The fear of failure can get to even the most seasoned experts. If you're not careful, you can fall into your own trap. You worry about failing, so you imagine all the horrible things that could happen if you fail. The intense worry causes bad stuff to happen, which becomes a self-fulfilling prophecy.

Pro Tip

Don't worry so much about failing —that you fail.

What Fear of Failure Feels Like

Metaphors are great tools to describe something you have a hard time putting words to. This is how I describe what the fear of failure feels like.

When I first grabbed hold of it—the fear of failure—it was just a pebble. It felt nice to have something to hold on to. It grounded me and made me feel safe. Over time it grew, but I felt secure and comfortable with my familiar rock. Others would comment about how nice it must be, and I hugged it with appreciation. Eventually, it got too big to take outside with me. I decided it was best to stay home and set it on my lap. It was more comfortable than having to carry it.

I didn't realize that staying indoors only made it grow bigger. I wanted to leave it behind to go out for a walk, but I couldn't move. Panic set in, and again I stayed put. The bigger the rock became, the more I shrank.

It became a huge rock, a boulder, if you will. Dark grey, cool to the touch, and heavy. So heavy I strained to hold it, and I pulled it close to me for better leverage. My breath became restricted as I shifted under its weight. My shoulders were all in knots. I couldn't seem to put this musty, dirty thing down. I couldn't see around it, and I was losing sight of my path. I wandered this way and that, and looked up to try to gain some clarity, but I became even more disoriented.

One day, my favorite client called to talk about a presentation he wanted me to deliver. My excitement turned to dread when reality sunk in. How would I present while holding onto this huge fear of failure? I was scared. What if the person they remember is no longer here? What if I traded all that I had been for the safety this rock provides? What if the part of me that is being called forth has been crushed beneath its weight?

I clung even tighter knowing I had a decision to make. I had to face fear completely exposed and vulnerable on my own—or I would continue to embrace the crushing comfort of safety until I became unrecognizable.

We are human, and we will fear failure. At times, it will be easier to succumb to failure than to embrace expansion. To give up or to give in can be easier than stepping out into the unknown with all the world's possibilities in front of you.

Pro Tip

**You must know for yourself:
Is it really the fear of failure or the fear
of expansion that haunts you?**

Here are three powerful ideas to move beyond the fear of failure:
1. Failure is your teacher. Be willing to learn.
2. Offer yourself grace. You are enough.
3. Breathe in possibility; breathe out fear.

What Expansion Feels Like

I had lived in the Minneapolis metro area for about ten years. My previous sales career had offered me the ability to explore a great deal of this beautiful city. A friend of mine had moved into a condo in one of the high-rise buildings downtown. I was invited to check out his new digs and was sufficiently impressed with his place, but then he took me to the top of the twenty-eight-floor building. As the rooftop door opened, I found myself awestruck with a spectacular 360-degree bird's eye view of the entire city. I've seen pictures to represent what I saw that night, but I've never experienced the cool breeze on my face, the glow of the sinking sun, the glittering city lights, and the infinite life energy that filled the streets. No cityscape has ever fascinated me and completely captured me this way.

I experienced that view not with my eyes but with my entire being. How long had I been walking at street level with only a brick wall in my sight line? How long had I been walking the same familiar sidewalks, confined by the buildings' ominous exteriors? How many times in life do we continue to walk the same path only seeing the same obstacles and render ourselves choiceless? That night, I was lifted as if on wings of an eagle to experience the limitless view of endless possibility. I saw what lies on the other side. I saw what lies in front and behind me. I saw all that I hadn't ever seen before. I saw the vast breadth of limitless opportunity. My world opened up because my perspective expanded.

Back on ground level, I now know what lies beyond the walls to the left and to the right of me. I know that life extends beyond what I have defined for myself. There is an entire world full of beauty and absolute possibility, and it's ready for me now. It's ready for you too. A new perspective is sometimes all you need.

♦♦♦♦♦

Speaker's Input:

When I was conducting a fraud-prevention seminar for about a hundred existing and prospective customers, I introduced one of my fellow presenters as my mom when I meant to say my manager. I responded by laughing at myself and injecting a comedic line. "I meant to say my work mom." My now-retired former manager said to me that it was the proudest moment of her career. We still keep in touch to this day, and now I simply refer to her as my other mother. I am grateful for that moment of embarrassment.

Kevin Pleasant, Senior Vice President, Treasury Management, MidWestOne Bank

♦♦♦♦♦

Chapter 6
Fear of the Audience's Power

"Your personal power is in the present." – Sara Krisher

The woman speaker took the stage with an over-the-top display of enthusiasm. Her explosive energy caught us all off guard. We sat in awe as she flung her arms this way and that. Her movement was sharp, and she danced with the words that poured out of her with the vigor of a fire hose. I could feel her setting up for the pause where the audience laughed on cue. *She has done this before*, I thought. She delicately shared a personal story, followed by an ask for sympathy. The audience responded in kind with teary eyes. I could tell the speaker was pleased. The amount of effort and time put into this highly polished presentation was admirable. But as well as the presentation was delivered, I couldn't help but feel distant and separate from the experience. I was touched by her story, and I appreciated the journey she took me on, but I still felt left out. As I walked out of the room, I reflected on what was missing. Why did her words not impact me or move me to change? After all, it was a great speech.

After some contemplation, I discovered what was missing. It was me. I was not part of the presentation. I sat in the audience and witnessed the performance as I would have a binge-worthy Netflix original. I watched, I was entertained, but I was not moved—and I was not changed.

I took time away from my work and had paid to be there. I had every intention of spending this time in this space with these people, and I walked away feeling a bit emptier and more confused than when I arrived. I hoped for clarity. I yearned for a breakthrough. I declared this would be the answer to my questions. It was not.

I didn't think I was alone. I might have been the only one finding words to describe it, but I couldn't have been the only one who walked away unfulfilled. By all accounts, the presenter was top-notch, the environment was ideal, and the topic was hot. There was just one problem. The speaker created the speech for herself. It was not for me or the person next to me or the person next to him. It was purposefully designed to validate the speaker. She could pat herself on the back for having dazzled the audience, and all the accolades afterward were sprinkles on the cake. She captured the moment with carefully positioned selfies for her social media profile following the speech. When the silence draws near and the walls close in, she will be scraping at the chance to speak again. It's an unhealthy relationship, and the cycle will continue.

Pro Tip

Gaining personal validation from the audience is a fleeting fullness that scurries away when the audience disassembles.

If you do that, you never quite know if you were successful, and you leave with questions. So, do not ask them if they like you. Do not speak to gain adoration or approval. Do not look to them as a child would a mother and plead to be worthy in their presence. Such an ask is not fair to them or you. You both deserve more.

The space at the front of the room is the gateway to a connected energy and meaningful shared purpose. The stage will take you by the hand and usher you through a highly connected relationship if you let it. It is a beautiful space reserved for you if you want it. The purpose of your message must be your north star. If you're able to connect, the audience will not judge you like you fear. Instead, they will ban together with you, and this connection will transcend judgment. Ultimately, it's your intentions that release you from the judgment you fear.

How to Connect with Your Audience

- **Speak your truth.**
  This incredible relationship begins with your presence and the beliefs you embody because they are communicated in your every move and revealed in your language. Every misalignment is spotlighted, so get clear on what you believe about your audience and your message.

- **Set aside your ego.**
  The relationship is strongest if you are willing to be of service to your audience. This means you seek to

understand what is important to them, and your message is crafted for them—not because they need you and you are God's gift, but because you're committed to this partnership. Who you are is not as important as who you are for them.

- **Seek to inspire.**
  Whoever said that hope is not a strategy didn't understand the power of emotion. We can have all the knowledge in the world, but without hope, we will not take action. Where there is no action, there is no change, growth, or improvement. It is hope that has us believing in something more for ourselves. Fueled hope turns into a dare to be and do more.

- **Select a worthy goal.**
  Many speakers make the mistake of having a goal that disconnects their words from their audience. The ego says, "I must be smart, credible, and know everything." This sends the speaker into a frenzy of research. They overload their presentation with facts and figures, and overwhelm their audience with heady knowledge and give little to no context of how or why the information is important. An assumption is made that the audience knows more than you, so you must overcompensate and impress. This alienates the audience and can turn them off to your message. All the time put into the preparation and delivery is wasted because it's fifty feet over their audience's

head. May I suggest you have a goal to connect to your audience?

Pro Tip

Choose a goal that draws you closer to the audience.

♦♦♦♦♦

Speaker's Input:

Like everything in life, practice makes perfect. You cannot practice too often. It builds confidence in what you are saying, and how you say it.
— Give your presentation to people you trust that will give you honest feed-back.
— Hear your voice and enunciate each word.
— Get comfortable with what you say and how you say it.
— Practice in front of a mirror.
— Watch your facial expressions as well as your body movements, and pay special attention to your body language.
— Make sure your body language fits your message.

- Be willing to change things, even if it's a little uncomfortable.
- Practice will make it comfortable.
- Give your presentation to people you trust that will give you honest feedback.

Prior to your presentation, get comfortable with your audience. Get there early. Meet people as they come in. Make friends. Get to know them; they become less intimidating, and they tend to get more engaged. Once you start your speech, make eye contact. Scan the audience and find the people most engaged in your message. If you find yourself in a tough spot, look for your "friends" in the audience—you'll find comfort and energy. Always remember they have no idea what you are supposed to say. If you forget something, don't worry! They haven't a clue. And then, HAVE FUN!

Bob Schlichte, Keynote Speaker and Former VP of Strategic Relationships at Grand Casino Mille Lacs/Hinckley

◆◆◆◆◆

Medusa

Hundreds of threatening beady eyes glaring right at me disturbed my sleep for weeks after seeing the movie *Clash of the Titans*. As a kid growing up in the eighties, I was terrified by the scene in the movie where the soldiers battle this creature named Medusa. She was a hideous female with greenish skin spouting venomous snakes for hair. Anyone who looked at her would instantly turn to stone. Even the strongest soldiers were no match for her.

Thankfully, as I became older, I realized Medusa was just a mythological character and could no longer pose a threat to me—or so I thought. I had just taken my place at the lectern and gently placed my notes in front of me. I lifted my head to glance out at the audience and instantly froze—turned to stone, if you will. As much as I had practiced and prepared, I didn't account for the audience's power. They were my modern-day Medusa.

What really happened that day? How did all the rehearsing and practicing disappear along with my presence of mind, leaving me to resemble a lifelike statue? I have a theory. Of course, hindsight is 20/20, and how could I have known I missed an especially important piece when preparing for my speech? I completely overlooked the importance of considering my audience. Yes, I knew who I was speaking to, and I knew what message I needed to get across, but I didn't know what I thought of them—and as a result, I imagined they were the enemy. They were separate from me. They were bigger and scarier and could crush me with a disapproving glare or challenging question. It was a truth I held inside. It wasn't something

I consciously created, and it completely stopped me in my tracks.

I realize now that the audience holds immense power. Rather than underestimate its strength or completely avoid it, I've learned to embrace it. A simple shift in perspective makes all the difference in turning my adversary into my advocate.

The following are my top five perspective-shifting tips for embracing your audience:

1. Imagine they are your partner, and you are working together.
2. Contemplate how you are similar and want the same things.
3. Seek to understand their struggle and put yourself in their shoes.
4. Invite them along rather than try to convince or persuade.
5. Assume best intentions and look for friendly faces.

♦♦♦♦♦

Speaker's Input:

No one is born with public-speaking skills. It's something that is developed over many years and experiences—the good, bad, and ugly ones. When I left my comfortable corporate job, I did not have any intention of being a speaker. Although I had given many presentations and facilitated many strategic conversations, I did not consider myself a speaker.

What changed for me was when I started doing more work in my passion areas. I couldn't help but share my passion, my opinions, my thoughts, and my ideas to help shift people's paradigms. And because of this passion, I started being asked to speak more and more. I realized that the best speakers are not the people who are most know-ledgeable on a topic. They are the people who are the most passionate about a topic, and they are able to convey that passion and message with words. They have the ability to share their passion in a way that shifts people's paradigms and makes them think differently.

Confidence in speaking comes from your passion. It comes from a place of wanting to share what you have learned, experienced, and believe in with the goal of having an impact on others. I have a completely different perspective now on what it means to be a speaker. I am much more fulfilled in my speaking opportunities because the experience gives me so much fulfillment. So, for me, that's what it truly means to have confidence in speaking.

—Jaime Adam Taets, Chief Vision Officer, Keystone Group International

♦♦♦♦♦

A New Approach

This sunny Saturday morning was a normal day with my seven-year-old daughter. We were getting ready for the day. We had plans for the afternoon, but it had been challenging convincing her to do the simplest things. But this was Saturday, and I was determined to have a stress-free day. We didn't have plans until 3:00 p.m., so I decided I would be patient but still hold my ground. I nonchalantly said, "Today is bath day," to which her response was, "NO!" She immediately started crying, so I was careful not to react. After all, this wasn't the first time she's gotten the better of me. She pleaded her case but couldn't move the mom rock. I kept my cool and explained that it wasn't worth the energy she was giving it. The bath would be quick and over before she knew it. She then stepped it up to more crying and shutting the door to her room. I remained patient. When she finally came out, I gave her two choices. She could take a nap, or she could take a bath. She got to decide. She then went into the bathroom and proceeded to lie on the floor next to the tub. *Well played,*

I thought. She was good. I began to wonder what type of reaction she wanted from me for her to put up such a fuss. Maybe she wanted me to get angry and hover over her until she got in the bath. Maybe she wanted me to give her some special attention? Maybe she wanted to see the vein in my forehead pop out while I all but threw her in the water.

I decided to try something new. I asked her to sit by me on the sofa. She reluctantly came over. When she sat next to me, I wrapped my arms around her and brought her to my lap. She was cradled in my arms like a big baby. I looked into her eyes, and I said, "I love you no matter what. You know that, right?"

She looked confused. I continued. "You're the best daughter I could ask for, and if I had the choice of all the daughters in the world, I would pick you. The strength that you are displaying right now is something I am very thankful to see in you. It will serve you in adulthood. Don't ever lose it."

She said she didn't understand. I went on.

"Your willful spirit is full of determination, and that's what you will need to get the things you want in life."

She asked, "Why isn't it working then?"

I smiled. "Because you are my daughter. You get that from me, and I am more determined to have you take a bath than you are not to."

She half-smiled, and I continued. "It's my responsebility as your mother to make sure you learn how to care for yourself so when you grow up and you are on your own, you know how to do the things you need to do for yourself. I take that responsibility very seriously. It would be so much easier for me to give in to you and let you make these types of decisions, but I would not be teaching you the valuable lessons." Her expression turned into understanding. "You are beautiful. You are strong. You are loved, and you belong. Don't ever doubt that. I love you when you are happy, and I love you when you are mad. I love you no matter what." We hugged and without another word, she took her bath.

Being a mother is more difficult than speaking. In the typical morning rush to get ready, I would not have had the patience and creativity to try something new. I had the presence of mind to be in the moment with my daughter, which allowed me to be at my best.

This experience encouraged me to think creatively about how I approach my audience when I'm challenged. They may not challenge me the way my seven-year-old did, but resisting and pushing aren't effective ways to get my point across.

Pro Tip

It's worth the extra time and attention required to come up with a creative way to influence audiences in a positive way.

Chapter 7
FEAR OF BEING SEEN

"People will forget what you said, people will forget what you did, but people will never forget how you made them feel." – Maya Angelou

I was a junior in high school the first time I stood my ground—the first time I stared in the face of all I feared and held my ground no matter what the consequences.

I was a new driver on a mission to get a friend a birthday gift in January in Iowa. January in Iowa is like living in an icebox. I didn't have a car yet, so I asked my mother if I could borrow hers. I got a block down the road and realized the gas gauge was pointing at E. I was convinced I'd be stranded on the side of the road any minute, and I had been working, so I had enough money to fill my mom's gas tank. I pulled into the gas station and noticed that the latch you pull to release the gas cap cover wasn't working. I thought there had to be a trick and started yanking on the latch, then walked around the car and yanked on the cover. It wouldn't budge. I pulled harder, and suddenly I felt it give. An optimistic thought was quickly replaced by dread. The cover didn't open.

Instead, I had pried the external cover from the unsightly metal cap. It still wasn't open, and now it was broken. I tried putting it back together with no luck. I asked the clerk if I could borrow the phone and call my mom. (This was before cell phones.) Mom answered, and I gently explained my good intentions, followed by a "please have mercy on me" confession. She was surprisingly understanding. She said not to worry, and I could still drive up to thirty miles when the meter displayed the tank was empty. Good information to know. Too bad I didn't know that earlier. Now I would be paying to fix her car.

I finished my errand and arrived home. As I exited the vehicle in the garage, I heard my stepfather yelling at the top of his lungs. This wasn't anything new, but this time, he was yelling at me and not my mom. I knew what it was about. Mom had told him I broke her car, and now he was going to make me pay. I could barely get in the house because he was blocking the door. I wasn't the frightened, shy girl I used to be when he would tower over me, and I'd cower. I was a resentful teenager. I was also full-grown and stood at 6'1". I'd had years to consider standing up to this monster. He screamed, "You are a disrespectful, destructive jerk! You have no respect for your mother or her property! You destroy everything you touch! You are nothing but a brute and have no consideration for anything or anyone!" He was so close to me I could feel the heat radiating from his red, bald forehead.

I told him that Mom and I already talked and that I had apologized and would fix the car with my own money. It wasn't good enough. He was exceptionally irate. He continued on and was staring into my eyes. I could feel his breath. I was sure he would hit me. I hadn't seen him be physically abusive, but I was always certain he was one provocation away from beating one of us. My mother was watching this word dual and tried intervening to no avail. I don't know what was going through Mom's mind, but for me, it was an out-of-body experience. For the first time, I was able to form thoughts as he berated me. I was able to consider my options. It was all happening in slow motion. I realized I was taller than him by a couple of inches. How had I not noticed before? That vein in his forehead suddenly looked like weakness to me. It was a crack in the beast. He yelled, "Go to your room!" I almost laughed. He thought he could command me like I was a younger version of myself. I taunted him. "Go to your room!" He reminded me that this was his house, and I would do what he said or leave. I told him to have a great life and put on my coat.

Mom convinced me to stay—and that was the last time I spoke to him. We continued to live in the same house for a year or more when Mom eventually divorced him, but it was never the same for me.

That day was the day I stepped out of the shadows. I pushed my fear aside. I stood my ground when I couldn't predict the outcome. I said to hell with the consequences. I got pushed to the edge, and I hung on. As I look back, I realize I was fortunate to have experienced this early in life. I learned where my power came from, and I knew what it felt like to bring it to the surface.

Pro Tip

**All of our experiences shape us.
No matter where yours have taken you, all your
stories have value.**

Don't dismiss the power and wisdom you have gained through the difficult times. They become the gold for navigating life and inspire us to rise above our experiences to design a life we desire.

It's Okay to be Seen

My brain has failed to produce vivid memories except when fear was present. One such time was when I was seventeen. I was shocked to be nominated for the role of president of the National Honor Society. Our family had just moved to the small Iowa town, and I started attending the high school a year prior. I didn't think anyone even noticed me. I was blown away when I found out I had been voted in as the president.

The role and responsibilities are blurred in the recess of my mind, but crisp outlines and bold colors bring one particular scene to life. As the new president, I was tasked with speaking in front of my peers and their parents. I don't remember the days leading up to the presentation, the preparation it must have taken, or the anxiety that might have hung over me like a cloud. The shrinking lens I use to look back includes only my walking to the stage and standing at the lectern.

I glanced up at the sea of peers and parents staring at me. I could feel the heat rising in my body, slowly at first, then suddenly it was like I was plunged into a hot dunk tank of fear and anxiety. My heart was pumping out of my chest, and I was certain the *thump, thump, thump* was being amplified through the microphone. Expectations and pressure wrapped around my neck so tight I could hardly breathe. It all happened so fast. I instantly felt exposed, judged, and paralyzed. I clung to the words on the page in front of me, and the rest of my speech is a blur.

I'm not alone in this kind of experience. Fear evokes protection. What was I really scared of that day? You may have picked up on it in my writing. I mentioned I had just moved to a new school and didn't think anyone even noticed me. I worked hard to blend in, to avoid attention, and to belong. It makes sense that stepping to the front of the room to deliver a speech to the very people I wanted to fit in with would terrify me. I would have to be confronted with being seen, which involved acceptance of *self*, and I hadn't even begun to figure out what that meant. I was still tripping over my growing feet and fighting my awkward 6'1" body. To protect myself, I hid behind the lectern, I clung to the pages in front of me and limited my eye contact. I was not present at all. I didn't consciously create the circumstances that served to protect me. All of it was orchestrated by the parts of me that kicked in when I was in need of hiding.

When I was learning to lead from the front of the room, I received lots of advice—not all of it was good. Maybe you've heard this before: Look at the back wall instead of the audience. While it is a strategy, it's catering to your fear.

Avoiding eye contact can cause the audience to question your intentions. They may think you are nervous, unprepared, or even disingenuous. But most of the time, it creates the impression that you are not confident, and if you are not confident in what you're saying, how can the audience be comfortable enough with your material to absorb it, and confident enough themselves to accept it?

Not only that, but you sacrifice connection with your audience when you squirm to avoid looking at them— and connection is the key to getting your message across! If you don't connect with your audience, you've just wasted your time and theirs, and your efforts were futile.

Pro Tip

Connection is the key to getting your message across. If you don't connect with your audience, you've just wasted your time and theirs, and your efforts were futile.

Looking someone in the eyes is an act of intimacy, connection, and acknowledgment. For a public speaker, *making eye contact means you are confident.* It reassures your audience of your credibility. Seeing the audience means you'll have to come out from hiding.

The truth is that the audience already sees you, whether you are looking at them or not; the question is: What will they see when they look at you? Doubt, fear, and uncertainty? Or confidence, strength, and assurance?

Which would you rather exude in front of your audience? You never get a second chance to make a first impression, so you must start strong, stay strong, and finish strong.

Your strength is expressed in your eye contact. If you find ways to avoid your audience, you will never develop the relationship you need to be influential, impactful, and get your message across.

So DO NOT take the stage trying to avoid being seen. Instead, accept that it is a privilege to be at the front of the room. You are powerful, and you do good work.

Pro Tip

Own yourself, own the room, own the material, and most importantly, own the moment.

The Audience's Perspective of Your Eye Contact

I am your audience. I see you. I see every bit of you. I see your polished shoes, your pressed suit, and your carefully combed hair. I see the subtleties in your gestures, your microexpressions, and I am witness to your every movement.

I am your audience and your judge and jury for the next hour. I will determine what I believe about you and your smart words. I will trust you, or I won't. I will follow you or fight you. What you do makes the difference. I am listening with my ears and fact-checking with my eyes. How you stand with your words will impact me or fall flat at my feet. How you choose your words will bring me closer to you or create a chasm. But most of all, how you see me will create either a champion or a villain—and then I'll respond that way.

When you look at me, do you shift uneasily? Do you squirm, and do your eyes hop from me to the floor? Do your eyes follow the pace of your hurried speech, skipping from person to person? Or, do your eyes dance in the moment and move to where they are needed?

Do you see me listening to you? Do you see me beyond how I show up in this moment? Do you see me as an extension of your vision, your ideas, and your efforts? Do you embrace me with your eyes because you want to partner with me as we head into the future?

Do you see me not because you were told to give good eye contact but because you are working to understand and meet my needs? Do your eyes land on me because you have lost yourself in this moment as you lead with purpose?

Can you abandon your fears and self-criticism, and join me where I am in the present with you? Can you really see me?

Authentic Expression

A confident presence is something we are all born with. It's something you learn to toss away, tuck away, and hide as we grow. We learn what others want from us. We're taught *how to be.* Our society and culture teach us what is considered safe and appropriate and what is not. We learn what others expect from us in work and in life, and we choose our battles. Over time, we realize it's easier to not fully express ourselves. We will make fewer waves if we keep our mouths shut. We'll please our bosses if we go along with what they say. In time, we sacrifice too much— at the expense of ourselves and the world. The world expects us to show up, whatever that means for you. If you believe the world expects you to show up fully, then you'll find ways to express yourself. You'll do what makes you come alive. You'll speak up, stand out, and step up when you are called to do so—not because it's what others expect from you, but because fully expressing yourself means living your life.

Pro Tip

Speak up, stand out, and step up when you are called to do so—not because it's what others expect from you, but because fully expressing yourself means living your life.

Hiding yourself from the world only brings feelings of doubt, shame, and avoidance. It seeps from your pores and detracts authenticity, trust, and connection. It brings with it a cloak of apology, wrapping itself around you to cover the shame inside. It rejects what makes you your awesome self and will only take you farther from confidence.

Authentic expression ought to be our goal. It's what makes us feel alive. It's what drives contribution. It's where confidence comes from, and it's available to every one of us. When we cultivate our personal gifts, talents, and strengths, we find it easier to fully express ourselves. Standing in that confidence means others will accept you. They will see your inner security and accept that you are speaking your truth. They will be attracted to you because you are alive. They will trust you because you trust yourself.

◆◆◆◆◆

Speaker's Input:

I was approached by an event planner to speak on communication and leadership for a national women's leadership conference in Minneapolis. A few days before the event, the planner let me know the conference would take place near the airport inside the retail store IKEA. I thought this was an unusual place to speak, and I quickly tried to visualize myself in a large conference room full of executive women—only to find out I was placed in the dining room section on the second floor. My audience was squeezed between dining tables and napkin rings.

While I was speaking, IKEA customers were shopping and asking me questions about where to find items. I had to laugh at myself and my situation as I was reminded of how important it is to be flexible in your presentations and to roll with the punches. These IKEA customer questions also offered numerous opportunities to add humor and key points to my stories. Remarkably, I received several spin-off speaking opportunities, and the overall conference was a huge success!

Diane Amundson, CEO at
The Thriving Workplace

♦♦♦♦♦

Chapter 8
FeaR OF BeinG HearD

"No matter what people tell you, words and ideas can change the world." – Robin Williams

I was envious of the Army brats when I was young because they had lived all over the world. Sure, they had to start new schools over and over, but at least they had a good excuse. Their parents were serving our country and making huge sacrifices to do it. My family moved all over Iowa, and I moved five times from the age of nine to the age of sixteen.

We moved to Spragueville, Iowa, when I was ten. It was a town of about three hundred people. Our closest neighbor was one mile down a gravel road. I didn't know how to initiate conversations, make friends, or even find someone to sit with at lunch. But that isn't the life-altering, shrink-in-my-seat, humiliating part of the story.

I hated math class. They were just wrapping up a unit on fractions, and at my last school, they hadn't even started fractions. I was not sure what a fraction was, let alone know how to add and subtract them. The teacher, I'll call him Mr. Bellows, was a large man with a booming voice and huge forearms.

I knew I didn't like him when one of my classmates was sick and had to leave class. As soon as she was out the door, he made fun of her, and the whole class laughed. This lumberjack of a man enjoyed making kids squirm.

One day, he called on me to answer a question. I wasn't sure I knew the answer, but I managed to squeak out a barely audible, "Forty-two." He asked me to repeat myself louder this time, so once again, I said, "Forty-two." He was just getting started with me. I felt hot all over, and everyone was staring at me. He ordered me to stand up and say it louder. I complied, saying, "Forty-two," in a way-louder voice than I was comfortable with. "Again," he said. Now I was mad. My embarrassment shifted to anger. How dare he humiliate me in front of all my peers. This time I yelled at the top of my lungs, "Forty-two!" and with a smirk, he said I could take a seat. He seemed satisfied with himself.

Mr. Bellows scared me into hearing myself loud and clear. I don't agree with his methods; however, that experience was so awful I never wanted to have to repeat myself again. From that point on, I answered questions loud enough to be heard, and whenever I was in his class, I yelled the answers. He seemed to like it.

The Fear of Being Heard comes from a timid and small place inside. If you are struggling to overcome this fear, here are some ideas to consider:

- Accept that you are worthy.
- Realize you have something of value to contribute.
- Take a stand for yourself—or nobody else will.
- Find ways to express yourself with your voice.
- Experiment with your volume, and get trusted feedback.
- Always use a microphone to amplify your voice when speaking to an audience.

That experience became a turning point for me. I had never heard myself speak above a soft-spoken whisper in school. I'm not sure how I would've grown out of the shy, quiet voice I became comfortable with had he not pushed me. Thanks a ton, Mr. Bellows.

Vocal Authenticity

If you've seen a typical business presentation, you've undoubtedly witnessed a phenomenon I like to call "The Talking Dead." You'll have to look really close to find the life behind the presenter's eyes, and if they are really good, you won't see or hear any vital signs. I'm not sure where this all started. Maybe at some point in history, someone with great credibility stood at the front of the room and bored the pants off the audience while aspiring business leaders watched and thought to themselves, *If I pretend I don't care and show no signs of life, I can deliver pre-sentations too!* That format multiplied, and now we have boring, lifeless, information-filled presentations.

Pro Tip

The goal of any presentation is to get a message to the audience.

First, the goal of any presentation is to get a message to the audience. The best way to do that is to make a connection. There are many ways to make a connection, and one way is through your voice—your natural voice—not a lifeless, monotone, business voice, a replication of someone else's, or even an exaggerated version of your own.

A term used by vocalists is *vocal authenticity*. Singers know when they get on stage to perform, they will be their most powerful when they use their own voice. They find it through experimentation, studying other artists, and connecting at a heart level with their words. It takes time for a new vocal artist to develop vocal authenticity. You'll be relieved to know I'm not suggesting you stand at the front of the room and belt out some notes to become a better presenter.

Instead, consider these three truths:

1. **When you withhold the life from your voice, you withhold your humanity, and you sacrifice connection.**
   Pay attention to your voice when you speak with your best friend, spouse, or parent. When you're in conversation with someone you hold in high regard, you instinctively express yourself using your voice. You might lower it when you are telling a secret or get really animated as you add drama to your story. As humans, we are great at expressing ourselves through story. The next time you engage in a juicy conversation, take notice of yourself. The voice you bring to that conversation is the voice you'll want to bring to the front of the room—the one where you talk with your hands, get your facial expressions involved, and naturally bring people along with you. You are interesting. You are relevant. You have what it takes. When you are present-minded and share a message the way you do, you're sharing a piece of you. Your audience appreciates you and what you have to offer.

2. **When you align your words, your actions, and your voice, you build trust.**
   Have you ever heard someone say, "I'm excited to be here today," but they look anything but excited. In fact, they look like they were forced at gunpoint to show up. Usually, those words come out at the

beginning of a presentation. It could be the first indication that the speaker can't be trusted. If what you are saying is not being expressed in your tone and your body language, your audience is left to wonder why. They may interpret this inconsistency as nerves, but if they can't see other signs of anxiety, they may decide you are lying. You set up your audience to be skeptical and challenge what comes out of your mouth. This is typically an unintended consequence of holding back. One of my clients described the eleven-second walk to the front of the room as if she were walking the plank, soon to be plunging to her death. The flood of energy and emotions that rise up is enough to create a foggy, frantic brain and leave us wanting to collapse or run away. The best way to get back to being you and to regain some composure is to breathe. When that doesn't work, breathe some more.

3. **Your voice is an extension of your beliefs.**
It's important to know what you believe about your audience, your content, and yourself when it comes to using your voice. As I shared in Chapter 3, I've been in an audience as the speaker decided to share her tips and tricks for being better, but in doing so, she used a tone just like my mother did when she was mad at me. She looked disappointed at times and shared common pitfalls with us as if we were idiots. I walked away from that

presentation feeling worse about myself for having listened to the speaker. I don't think this was her intent, but her beliefs about the audience were coming out in her tone, pitch, and words. Be sure to get clear on your beliefs before you present because they drive your thoughts, which drive your actions at the front of the room.

Pro Tip

Find a way to view your audience as your friend not your foe.

◆◆◆◆◆

Speaker's Input:

I was speaking at a church service one Sunday morning and had everything ready to go. I arrived early, I had my notes, and I got my microphone all set up. When it was time, I jumped up on stage and started talking, but there was no sound. The people in the back couldn't hear a word I was saying.

The pastor jumped up and told me to keep talking while he kneeled next to me and fiddled with the mic box affixed to my hip. My rhythm was off now, and how I had planned to open was thrown out the window. I started improvising as he worked. I made jokes. "Can you hear me now?" "Hey, what's up?" Unfortunately, my microphone was broken.

They gave me a hand-held mic to use, which I was not planning on using. One of my demonstrations was of me juggling, which is much more challenging while you're holding a hand-held mic! In the end, I used my sense of humor to keep it light and get myself back on track.

I learned that day that speaking in front of an audience is more about showing up authentically and rolling with what happens and less about needing every word and detail to go just as planned.

Danielle Allen, Owner and Coach at One Foot Coaching & Consulting

♦♦♦♦♦

Introverts Make Great Public Speakers

I encounter this all the time. The look of concern and apprehension as my client confesses to me that they are an introvert. Their eyes tell me: "I'm sorry. This isn't going to be easy. I sure hope you are up for the challenge." They go on to express all their fears regarding speaking to groups and how they've been avoiding the traumatic experience that is sure to ensue. They are afraid they won't be any good, but their gut is telling them that if they don't take action, they will regret it.

While they are inclined to speak less on average, I am pleased to dispel the myth that introverts can't be good at speaking to audiences. I have witnessed incredible speakers who captivate me from the beginning, engage me throughout and leave me inspired to act. In talking with these amazing speakers, they openly admit their introverted status. (Usually with the caveat that they will need to retire to their hotel room as soon as possible after their gig to recharge in true introvert fashion.)

Here are the Top Five Reasons Introverts are Great Public Speakers:

1. They won't speak to an audience unless they have something of value to pass along.
What an introvert has to say must be more important or more valuable than the discomfort they will have to go through to share it. This means they spend the time to contemplate why their message matters. By the time they take the stage, there is a darn good reason for it.

2. They enjoy the thoughtful, quiet space and time needed to prepare for a presentation.
Let's face it. Introverts like being alone because it refuels them. The process of preparing a great presentation requires alone time. The writing,

researching, and organizing are all providing them with energy. It's fun for them—and the audience benefits.

3. They are succinct and purposeful with their word choice.

When an introvert is ready to deliver a presentation, they have completely contemplated every which way the topic could be communicated. They've thought of the pitfalls, the advantages, and everything in between. They are deliberate and have thought through the talk from start to finish, leaving nothing to chance.

4. Their passion comes from a deep, meaningful place.

Introverts don't speak for the limelight or the attention. They are driven by passion, responsibility, or purpose. They are reflective and work hard to create a great presentation. They are open to feedback and are interested in the audience's experience. They are not speaking for themselves. They are sharing a message the audience needs to hear.

5. The audience trusts them because they know they go deep with their topic.

Introverts loath small talk. They are great listeners and observers. When they communicate, they like to communicate truth. They have evidence to back up their claims, and they can cite the source. They don't make assumptions. They test theories and measure outcomes. They take their status of "expert" seriously and go deep to learn as much as possible. They won't let something they say lead you astray.

So, if you are inclined to recharge in solitude, be assured you have what it takes to be great at public speaking. You are uniquely qualified to make a powerful impact at the front of the room.

Turn Them into Active Not Passive Listeners

Tonight, he shared another nugget of wisdom. My daughter's voice instructor was praising Danika for doing a wonderful job on a song. She was singing "I Dreamed a Dream" from *Les Misérables*. He told her she sang it beautifully. He even liked it more than the version done by the woman who sings it in the movie. That was flattering, but what came next was fascinating. He stopped, turned himself towards her, and changed into the wise teacher. He said that sometimes in an attempt to express emotion, a singer will turn their audience into watchers. He said that there is a space you can strive for that shows enough emotion to allow the audience to participate in the emotion.

That's it, I thought. In the same way, when a speaker turns into the entertainer, we turn our audience into passive listeners instead of actively participating. Brilliant.

As speakers, our main concern ought to be the audience's experience. How we connect with them matters. It will touch them intrinsically, so the knowledge is absorbed rather than lost forever.

Pro Tip

As speakers, our main concern ought to be the audience's experience.

Chapter 9
YOUR AUDIENCE IS WAITING

"Change will only happen when brave people speak up."
– daughter, Danika Socwell

A dear friend of mine was offered the opportunity to present to a high-achieving group of individuals from an international company. The presentation had to be customized and delivered with great care, but she had only three weeks. She accepted the challenge and called me up right away. She wanted to know if I would accompany her on the trip to the Florida Keys. Umm, yes! The caveat was I would need to play a big role in making sure she was prepared for her talk, and that she had the support she needed in the days leading up to the event.

We worked hard to prepare. She spent a good deal of time considering all the things that could go wrong. We analyzed her content and scrutinized her words. She created a masterpiece to share and began practicing. The anticipation occupied every moment of our time until she delivered the speech.

The day of the presentation, I waited in the sun until her talk was over. Initially, she was relieved. We were both so glad it was over. "How did it go?" I asked. She said it went well, and although they were slow to engage, she was happy she was able to get them talking. Overall, she was pleased.

Within the hour, her adrenaline gave way to self-doubt. She was reflecting back on the subtleties of the audience's facial expressions and their responses to questions, and she was playing back parts of the speech that could have been better. Her upbeat demeanor was soon replaced with a defeated posture. She began to consider what she should have said—and began to beat herself up for the slightest infractions.

What she was going through is completely natural. I've done it myself, and I've observed hundreds of presenters enter this dark zone after the talk is over. Initially, the adrenaline from "bringing it" protects you from what is to follow, which is the inevitable let down. It happens the hour after the talk is done. Everyone goes back to work. The room is empty. You've moved on. You start to question.

- How did it really go?
- Did they mean it when they said they liked my presentation?"
- They probably said it to be nice.
- Come to think of it, nobody asked me any questions afterward.
- Nobody took me up on my offer.
- In fact, I saw one person yawning and another half-asleep while I was presenting.

– I did a terrible job. It was awful, and that's what the evidence supports.

The dark zone is a confidence killer and erodes opportunities for future success at the front of the room by perpetuating the fear of failure.

We were seated at an outdoor bar as she entered the dark zone of self-doubt. Fortunately, her audience had just been let out of their meeting and had to walk by her to get where they were going. I saw person after person stop, shake her hand, and thank her for her thought-provoking, powerful, incredible talk. She looked at me as if to ask if that had really happened. I fear if I hadn't been there, she might have thought she dreamed it.

What is the Appropriate Measurement of Success When Presenting to an Audience?

A colleague of mine lives for the standing ovation. And another focuses on how many consulting gigs she walks away with. I used to think that if I had someone come up afterward to talk to me, that was a sign of success. Unfortunately, there have been many times I finished presenting, and nobody came up to talk to me. I had to reevaluate my measurement of success. Now, I tend to measure a job well done in terms of connection behaviors. If I get good eye contact from my audience, and they engage with me and answer my questions, I believe that is a good indication of success.

It may be different for each presenter, but we would be wise to consider what will tell us this presentation was successful when it's all said and done. It will help us navigate around the dark zone. I also caution you to shut off the inner voice that starts criticizing you an hour after it's over. You can analyze your talk later, but this is the worst time to do it.

How Can You Tell if You've Engaged Your Audience?

- Complied with your requests
- Nodded their heads
- Laughed when appropriate
- Engaged in cross discussion when appropriate
- Participated throughout your presentation
- Gave you feedback
- Approached you after the presentation
- Fulfilled your call to action
- Referred you
- Connected with you afterward

Thank You, Coach McNeill

When I was sixteen, my family moved to a small town in Iowa halfway through the school year. It wasn't the first time I had to make new friends and start from scratch, but I admit I was intimidated by the small class sizes. I quickly integrated because I joined the basketball team. It was midway through the season, which was quickly coming to a close. I was told there was a parents' night, but I didn't think it was a big deal. I mean, I imagined a bunch of parents and a potluck dinner.

I told my mom about it, but she was exhausted from work, and I didn't want to force her to mingle over little wieners and meatballs. My father lived a couple of hours away, so he wasn't able to make it. In my oblivious teenage fashion, I showed up for the parents' night only partially interested. My eyes widened when I realized there weren't just parents but entire families showing up to this thing— brothers, sisters, aunts, uncles, and grandparents all filing into the bleachers. I was horrified. It looked as if they were all about to watch some sort of show, and just then, I spotted the lectern centered in the gym. I started rationalizing. It looked like we would be recognized in front of our families. *No big deal*, I thought. Nobody needed to know my family wasn't there.

As we lined up for our trek across the gym floor to get recognized, I realized that the moms and dads were escorting each of my teammates across the stage! I had no mom or dad—and I was the only one. My heart sunk. Anxiety filled my lungs, and I started to panic. Why had I not made a bigger deal of this night? Why did I have no clue what to expect? Why am I sixteen, all alone in a gymnasium full of other people's caring family members?

Names kept being called as another set of proud parents walked the sweet apple of their eye across the floor while the audience cheered and clapped. My mind frantically ran through escape scenarios. I could run out the back door. I could fake being sick and run out of the front door. Oh why, oh why was I going to be humiliated in front of all of these people?

Just then, my name was called. I froze. Suddenly, I felt an arm lock in mine, and a man led me across the gym floor. The man was the father of the teammate behind me. I looked back and saw her mother nod me off as if to say, "Go on, I will walk my daughter out." The man that rescued me from crushing embarrassment was Coach McNeill. He was the boys' basketball coach, so I didn't know him well. How did he know how desperate I was to be rescued at that very moment? How did he know I wanted someone to save me from the humiliation of a lonely walk across that stage? How did he know to grab my arm in that moment? I will forever be grateful for his intervention.

Not only did Coach McNeill's act of kindness that day warm my heart and bail me out of an absolutely agonizing situation, but it greatly impacted my life. The difference he made echoes through me and has had a ripple effect on the next generation. I want to make a difference like that one day. I keep my eyes open for the opportunity to be the one to walk with someone in a time of need. I became a life coach for this reason. I know it also affects and impacts my daughter. She sees my example, the example set for me all those years ago. A thoughtful gesture in a moment in time can make all the difference in a person's life. I have Coach McNeill to thank for that gift.

Every time you speak, you have the opportunity to make a difference in another person's life. If you think that all you are doing is offering information, I beg you to reconsider. You have wisdom only you have gained. If you're like me, you've learned it the hard way. Only you can share this wisdom by being willing to speak your truth.

♦♦♦♦♦

Speaker's Input:

I was in Vancouver speaking for a huge speaker-industry conference. I had to be on stage in 45 minutes for five hundred people who were waiting for me to talk to them about showing up as your best self even when life is stressful. But my head was in my hotel room toilet expelling my stomach's contents due to some sort of stomach bug—and no, it wasn't nerves or a hangover! It's kind of funny and ironic that my topic was exactly what I needed to tap into for my own success that day!

Over the years, I've experimented with how to maintain my body and brain—biohacking if you want to get scientific! That day I knew I needed to stabilize my stomach, soothe my acid-ripped throat, and get my brain clear so I could deliver a top-notch speech—or at least show up for it and not totally stink up the joint (or puke on stage)! Enter peppermint oil, honey, and olive oil gargle and a set of yoga moves to activate my brain and de-active my stomach! I certainly wasn't my very best on stage that day, but I did get some spin-off business, so I didn't suck as badly as I could have had I not been open to experimentation to ensure that no matter what happened before speaking, I could still maximize my body and brain to show up as I intend.

Kristen Brown is a keynote speaker, biohacker, bestselling author, and energy mastery expert who charges up her clients by syncing up their body, mind, and spirit for work and life growth. Learn more at www.KristenBrownPresents.com and www.namaSync.com.

◆ ◆ ◆ ◆ ◆

Pro Tip

The key to confidence is preparation and knowing what YOU need to be your best no matter what!

Resilience Required

My daughter had a track and field day at school when she was ten. It was in the middle of the day, and I was glad to be able to be there. You could feel the excitement in the air. The kids were pumped and ready to give it their all. They were nervous because their peers would be watching.

I took my seat on the lawn and watched the first group run as fast as they could while jumping over hurdles. One girl caught her foot on a hurdle and fell. She didn't get back up. She was crying and had to be escorted off the field. My heart went out to the girl as I'm sure she was crying just as much from embarrassment as any pain she felt.

Life went on and so did the next race. It wasn't ten minutes later that the same thing happened to another girl. I expected her to wait for a sympathetic teacher to help her up—half-expecting that there was a new protocol for falling that required you to stay down and wait for help to arrive. This time, however, the girl popped back up and took off. She looked more determined than ever and gave it her all to get across that finish line.

My daughter told me later that the first girl who fell is known as the fastest girl in school. She always performed well, and she had the ego to prove it. Everyone was shocked that she fell, including her. The other girl was known as a tough girl. She was bigger than a lot of the kids. There was no expectation in their minds that she would be the fastest. It was no surprise to my daughter that the second girl got back up and kept going because what she lacked in speed, she compensated with determination. She didn't win the race, but she finished with her head held high.

This was a real-time display of resilience playing out before my eyes. I thought, *Doesn't this happen to us in life every day?* We have opportunities, we give it our all, and we stumble and fall. We get to choose whether we keep going with determination or let failure keep us from ever reaching the finish line.

I won't tell you that speaking will always end in success, but I promise you it will always teach you what you are meant to learn.

You Are Worth It

Her voice was desperate when she called. I knew whatever came next would be important. My younger sister Amy wears her heart on her sleeve, so I never have to guess what she is thinking or feeling. She tells it like it is, and she is full of expressive energy.

She needed my advice. She moved to Florida from Wisconsin after her divorce a few years earlier and was now ready to buy a house. She found the perfect one in her price range. It didn't require any money down, and nobody had ever lived in it. It had a beautiful open floor plan, marble countertops, brand new appliances, three bedrooms, and a great backyard.

The realtor had explained that the financing fell through for the couple that was supposed to move in. It was within the first twenty-four hours, and if Amy waited to carefully weigh her decision, the house would be gone. She had to make what felt like a split-second decision.

Buying a house is not something one does on a whim. Being it was a huge decision to make, it was best to have your older sister weigh in. "What should I do?" she whispered into the phone. I replied, "It sounds awesome. What is the drawback?" She couldn't think of any reason other than it seemed too nice. She didn't think she deserved such a nice house and couldn't imagine herself in it. She started crying when she heard herself say the words. She knew that was not a reason to let go of such a great opportunity. When we were growing up, we never had a lot of money. We learned to be responsible and practical with our money, so anything extravagant seemed out of reach and not for us.

When she made the decision to buy the house, *she also had to make the decision she was worth it.* When we step out of our comfort zone to do something big, it can feel like a huge risk. We will be presented with fantastic decisions. That's what makes life exciting. You are worth it, and you are meant for great things. Always remember that.

Acknowledgments

Thank you to my daughter Danika Socwell. The day you were born you became my greatest experiment, my most valuable lesson, and my strongest connection. Thank you for waking me up to my earthly mission.

To my husband Neal Krisher, who has shown me the sides of myself I was afraid to see. You've taught me how to recognize my worth and embrace it. Thank you for being my biggest fan, my best friend, and my steady place to land when it all gets to be too much.

To the best storyteller and creator I've ever known, Jennie Antolak, whose friendship and wisdom astound me. You've taught me how to listen to my inner wisdom and follow its lead. Your life's work at Learning Journeys International Center of Coaching transformed me and changed the trajectory of my life. I wouldn't be living my purpose if it weren't for you. Thank you for being my thought partner, my cherished friend, and for always making me laugh.

To Scott Plum, because when I first met you, one of the questions you asked me is, "How is your faith?" You continually challenge me, and it was you who reintroduced me to my higher power. If it weren't for you, I wouldn't be taking risks and having faith that it will all work out.

To my sister Amy Davis. Thank you for being my champion, especially when the chips were down. You always know how to lift me up and when to kick me in the pants. I appreciate your unconditional love. Your friendship means the world to me, and you are the best virtual assistant a business owner could ask for.

To my audience, it's my hope that this book will unlock something in you, and you will set it free with your voice. Please remember the following:

- Your words become your truth, and you stand firmly in them while courageously saying what needs to be said—not because you have to deliver a presentation but because you are called to make an impact in only the way you can.
- Bravely share your ideas, your thoughts, and your knowledge, and trust that it will land on your audience and awaken them to possibilities.
- Each time you speak, you inspire hope because hope leads to action, and anything else is simply not enough.

To my publisher, Kirk House Publishers. Ann, you made this process seamless and fun. Thank you for making one of my dreams come true.

To my editor, Connie Anderson, at Words & Deeds, Inc. You get me, and you make me look good. Thank you from the bottom of my heart.

About the Author

Sara Krisher is the president and founder of STAND TALL, a company that helps build confidence. Her extensive work in business-to-business sales and public speaking training has been developed from her twenty-plus years' experience presenting to Fortune 500 companies and small to medium-size businesses.

She is an international speaker, narrative coach, and developer of the "Fearless Speaker" program. She delivers training programs to business leaders who want to lead from the front of the room with more confidence.

Sara's passion for speaking her truth is evident in her candid approach to communications. Her clients like her fun, spirited, and encouraging personality. She is a champion of bravery and doesn't just *talk the talk*. She continually demonstrates confidence building in her work and personal life. She stands tall at 6'1" and looks up to her fourteen-year-old daughter, who is 6'2" tall. You can learn more about her services at STANDTALL.com